T0078053

GROWING FAITH DURING DIFFICULT TIMES

GEORGE E PFAUTSCH

authorHOUSE®

AuthorHouse™
1663 Liberty Drive
Bloomington, IN 47403
www.authorhouse.com
Phone: 833-262-8899

Published by AuthorHouse 10/14/2021

ISBN: 978-1-6655-4124-4 (sc)
ISBN: 978-1-6655-4123-7 (e)

Library of Congress Control Number: 2021921238

CONTENTS

Growing Faith

INTRODUCTION

There are many situations and actions in our world today that can easily lead us to believe we are living at a time when evil is more prevalent than it has ever been. Hatred and divisiveness all too frequently are being substituted for love of God and neighbor.

In reality, all human beings have lived through diabolical times. From the time Satan (serpent) tempted and persuaded Eve in the Garden of Eden to eat of the forbidden fruit, evil has existed in the world.

Dealing with evil is a struggle for human beings. It can become an even greater struggle when society accepts and endorses evil practices. In our Church and in our Nation, there have been questionable practices, some of which are accepted by our society, that make it more difficult to maintain or increase our faith in God. We will examine a few such evils in this book.

God did not leave us without a blueprint for combating evil. In the Old Testament he gave Moses the Ten Commandments. In the New Testament our Savior tells us of the two greatest commandments.

First, we are to love our God with all our heart, soul, mind, and strength and secondly, we are to love our neighbor as our self. It is through the departure from these commandments that we open the door to evil. It is through love, and especially through love of God and his commandments, that evil is overcome.

We will look at periods of times and actions which were and are diabolical. Why our Lord seems to permit Satan to be more intrusive at times is mysterious and will continue to be mysterious after this book is written. But we will look at those time periods and situations and attempt to assess how many good and holy people lived through such periods and remained faithful and also grew in faith during them.

At the present time our Church suffers from a lack of participation in the practice of the Catholic faith and in a lack of belief in the Real Presence of the Holy Eucharist. The proclaimed reasons for that are numerous. My own view is that both situations relate primarily to a lack of faith. The reasons for that will be reviewed at more length in this book.

It is not only some members of our Church who lack faith, but such a lack of faith also applies to a large number of people in our nation. Hatred and divisiveness have become trademarks within our government and our news media. That in turn tends to spread to a growing number of our citizens. The causes for that will also be assessed at greater length later in this book.

It may seem simplistic to attribute all the historical and current evils of societies to a lack of faith and more specifically to a lack of love of God and neighbor. Nevertheless, it is my firm conviction and my simple view that it happens to be the simple truth. A greater love of God and neighbor would eliminate much of the evil that has occurred in the world and that continues to occur. A perfect love of God would eliminate all such evil. Such perfection will have to await our arrival into his Kingdom.

Unfortunately, God did not create perfect humans. Rather, He created humans who are sinners. It does seem that there have been periods and situations when diabolical intrusions have been more severe. As previously noted, it is the purpose of this book to explore such periods and try to better assess why they occur.

CHAPTER 1

HISTORICAL DIABOLICAL INTRUSIONS

I n the first Chapter of the Biblical Book of Genesis, we are told of God's Creations, and that God created man in his image. Nevertheless, from the earliest days following creation, we have examples of diabolical intrusions into humanity.

In Chapter 3 of Genesis we are told of the initial satanical intrusion. After God created Adam and Eve and settled them in the Garden of Eden, he gave them this command; *You are free to eat from any of the trees of the garden except the tree of knowledge of good and bad. From that tree you shall not eat; the moment you eat from it you are surely doomed to die.* As we know, following the urging of the serpent (Satan) Eve and Adam both ate of the fruit from the tree of knowledge. With that first sin, humans have been guilty of the original sin of pride, whereby we set aside the commands of our Lord and subject ourselves to the temptations of the devil.

Genesis also tells us of the sins of Cain and Lemech. The additional sins of early created humans led to God's regret in creating humans, which in turn led to the great flood that destroyed many of the humans God had created. But in the story of Genesis we are also told that Noah, a son of Lemech, found favor with the Lord. We know the story of the ark Noah built and the preservation of the human race. We are told that Noah observed all the commands God gave him. The story of Noah is also the story of how faith in God, is the remedy to deal with diabolical intrusions. The important moral lesson of the story of Noah is the importance of faith in the midst of evil.

The book of Genesis also gives us the story of Abraham. It was with great faith that Abraham left the land of his kinsfolk and went to the land where our Lord asked him to go. As with Noah, Abraham observed the command our Lord gave him. Early in Chapter 15 of Genesis we are told that the Lord told Abraham in a vision, "I will make your reward very great".

The message of Genesis is a simple message from our God. My commands are simple requests of obedience. For those who were not obedient, punishment took place. For those who obeyed them, He made their reward "very great".

The story of good and evil is advanced in the Old Testament Book of Exodus. On the 40-year trek from slavery in Egypt to the land of Israel there are numerous stories of great rewards from God. They included the parting of the Red Sea, the delivery of manna in the desert and water from the rock. Through these signs, the people would be thankful to God and praise Him. But Exodus also tells us stories of diabolical intrusions. The lack of gratitude often disappeared during times of hardship. The Israelites also turned to false gods, including the molten golden calf, during the journey. Throughout the forty years, Moses maintained his faithfulness.

During the journey, God expanded his commands for humans, by providing Moses with the Ten Commandments. It was early in the journey out of Egypt when the Israelites reached the Sinai desert. During that period God summoned Moses to the top of Mount Sinai where he gave Moses the Ten Commandments. Through these commandments, God provided his people a more comprehensive set of rules to indicate the love of their Creator. As with future generations of humans, these commands were broken when in their sinful pride, they looked toward diabolical intrusions rather than the Word of God.

But a merciful God would go much further to show his compassion for the people He created. Long after the time of Exodus, He would send his Son to live amongst us to provide us with greater revelations of the Father and who would demonstrate his ultimate love for humans by suffering and dying on a Cross to redeem their sins.

Jesus gave us the two greatest commandments. Matthew 22 – 34-40 provides us with those words; *When the Pharisees heard that he had silenced the Sadducees, they gathered together, and one of them (a scholar of the law) tested him by asking, "Teacher, which commandment in the law is the greatest?" He said to him, "You shall love the Lord, your God, with all your heart, with all your soul, and with all your mind. This is the greatest and the first commandment. The second is like it: You shall love your neighbor as yourself. The whole law and the prophets depend on these two commandments."*

There are few words in the Good News that are any clearer than the above. Our purpose on earth is to love God above all else and to love our neighbor as our self. Even though He told us that His yoke is easy and His burden is light, we flawed humans transgress daily from those words. Our sinful pride (the basis of all diabolical intrusions) leads us away from those words all too often. His words are words that should lead us to frequent prayer. A friend of mine once told me that the one time we humans do not sin is when we pray. It is a good reason that we should pray constantly. If we pray constantly, we will grow in faith despite the diabolical intrusions that surround us.

Our Savior taught us much about love during his time on earth. His entire purpose on earth was a message of love. When we spend more and more time concerned with that message of love, the more we grow in faith. We have no excuses. There is no diabolical intrusion that can force us away from loving him. He gave us a free will. It is up to each of us to grow in faith.

During his time on earth, even those close to Him did not follow his words perfectly. Peter denied Him three times before the cock crowed. Thomas would not believe our Lord had risen until he touched the wounds. The mother of James and John wished for her sons to be seated at his right and his left when they entered his Kingdom. We will never reach the level of perfect love during our time on earth, but each of his can strive daily for a higher level of faith.

Our Lord not only gave us the two greatest commandments during his time on earth. He gave us the Beatitudes which are set forth in the 5th chapter of Matthew:

Blessed are the poor in spirit, for theirs is the kingdom of heaven.
Blessed are they who mourn, for they will be comforted.
Blessed are the meek, for they will inherit the land.
Blessed are they who hunger and thirst for righteousness, for they will be satisfied.
Blessed are the merciful, for they will be shown mercy.
Blessed are the clean of heart, for they will see God.
Blessed are the peacemakers, for they will be called children of God.
Blessed are they who are persecuted for the sake of righteousness, for theirs is the kingdom of Heaven.

When diabolical intrusions tempt us, the words of the Beatitudes can help keep us on the right path.

The Bible is indeed properly referred to as "The Good News". It was and continues to be the book that shows us the Way, the Truth and the Life.

Before closing this chapter, I would like to refer to an incident Jesus encountered with his disciples and which is a good way to measure how we have grown in faith. It comes at the end of the Bread of Life Discourse found in the 6th Chapter of John.

Amen, amen, I say to you, whoever believes has eternal life. I am the bread of life. Your ancestors ate the manna in the desert, but they died; this is the bread that comes down from heaven so that one may eat it and not die. I am the living bread that came down from heaven; whoever eats this bread will live forever; and the bread that I will give is my flesh for the life of the world."

The Jews quarreled among themselves say, "How can this man give us his flesh to eat?" Jesus, said to them, "Amen, amen I say to you, unless you eat the flesh of the Son of Man and drink his blood, you do not have life within you. Whoever eats my flesh and drinks my blood has eternal life, and I will raise him on the last day. For my flesh is true food, and my blood is true drink…

John 6 goes on to tell us that because of the above words many of his disciples did not have the faith to believe his words and left Him and would no longer accompany Him.

On the night of the Last Supper when He instituted the Holy Eucharist, He told his apostles to "Do This in Memory of Me". One of the primary reasons I am a Catholic has to do with my belief that the gifts of bread and wine are truly transubstantiated into the Body and Blood of our Lord at the Consecration of each Mass.

It is unfortunate that many Catholics do not have the faith to believe in the Transubstantiation. Our Church reminds us that it should not be any more difficult to believe in the Transubstantiation than it is to believe that God could create our Universe from nothing.

Many spiritual beliefs are a matter of our faith. None of those beliefs are of greater spiritual value to us than is the belief of the Real Presence in the Holy Eucharist. It is a great defense against diabolical temptations.

CHAPTER 2

PRE-REFORMATION CHURCH

T he Church had to survive many struggles during its formative early years. Many of those struggles are provided in the Gospels and in the Acts of the Apostles. While Christianity spread rapidly after our Lord's Ascension, it did so through many adverse conditions.

All but one of the Apostles were martyred. Many of the faithful who followed them would also be martyred. Christianity and faith in God were no doubt considered a threat to many early secular world leaders.

A number of Roman Emperors were among those who would persecute Christians. We cannot understand all the motives for the persecutions but as already noted, the threat to their authority, along with their lust for power were among the likely reasons.

Nero was the Roman Emperor at the time Peter was crucified upside down. It was also Nero who blamed Christians for the Great Fire that occurred in 64 AD. Nero punished Christians by crucifixion, and by other even crueler means. His persecutions set a precedent and being a Christian was reason enough for some form of capital punishment.

Other Roman Emperors were among those who persecuted Christians and one of the worst was Marcus Aurelius, who became Emperor in 161 AD. Decius, the Roman Emperor from 201 AD to 251 AD became the first Emperor to organize persecutions of Christians throughout the Roman Empire. Christian persecutions were continued by Diocletian who became Emperor in 284 AD.

These persecutions ended in 306 AD when Constantine became Emperor. With the Edict of Milan, which he signed in 313 AD, he gave Christians and others the freedom of religion.

Despite the persecutions of Christians, it is believed that the number of believers were somewhere between five and six million at the time Constantine came to power. At the end of his reign the Christian population is believed to have grown to almost 30 million. Constantine, whose mother Helena was a Christian and declared a saint, himself became a Christian. The growing number of those who became Christians during his reign is a legacy to his faith. He not only embraced the faith himself, but enabled millions of others to embrace and grow their faith.

From the first Pope, Peter, to the time Constantine became Emperor, thirty Popes would lead the Catholic Church. Not a great deal is known about many of these

Popes, but they led the Church during difficult times, and several were martyred.

The Church in its early days was also subjected to some heresies, as the Church struggled to define itself, and to better define our Savior and his Mother. Constantine himself summoned a Council in Nicaea of the important bishops of that time. The Council was summoned because of a heresy by a priest from Alexandria, Egypt who taught that God the Father existed before the Son and that therefore the Son must be less than the Father. The Bishops not only dispelled that teaching but also defined the faith in what we now know as the Nicene Creed.

Several additional Ecumenical Councils were held by the Church in its first 500 years. Because of their significance in establishing important tenets of our Catholic faith, we will mention them.

The Council that followed the Council in Nicaea was the First Council of Constantinople which was held in 381 AD. The most important issue of that Council was to clarify the role of the Holy Spirit in the Blessed Trinity. That role was added to the Nicene Creed.

After the First Council of Constantinople, came the Council of Ephesus which was held in 431 AD. An important issue of that Council was to declare that Mary was the Mother of God (theotokos) and not merely the Mother of Christ in his humanity.

At the Council of Chalcedon, it was declared that Jesus Christ was truly God and Man. It was an important decision and is still specifically included when we recite the Divine Praises. It was important because it remains a difficult belief until this time. That Council effectively stated that the two natures of Jesus should not be viewed separately. It specifically stated that the Son of God had two natures which "should be acknowledged without confusion, division, change or separation". That is difficult for many to do. From a personal perspective, this confession by the Church regarding our Lord's two natures is the apex of Christology.

The Councils of Nicaea, Constantinople and Chalcedon were all convened to clarify heresies that had arisen. For me personally, it is not difficult to understand that some "heresies" might arise as the early Church was struggling to define what today we accept as matters of faith and morals. Therefore, it is not my view that the "heresies" of the early Church were as much diabolical as they were struggles to define the truth.

During those struggles of Christological definition, the papal chair was filled by one of our early great Popes, who was one of only two to be given the title of "Great". Pope Leo 1 was elected in the year 440 AD and died on November 10, 461 AD. He was the pope during the Council of Chalcedon which was held in 451 AD. He was the author of the Tome of Leo which laid the foundation for the Christological conclusions reached at the Council of Chalcedon. Pope Leo was also credited with confronting Attila the Hun and convincing him not to lay siege to Rome. Pope Leo was also instrumental in establishing Papal Supremacy.

Another prominent theologian of the early Church was St. Augustine (354 AD – 430 AD). Two of his written works "Confessions" and "City of God" are theological masterpieces. A personal reason for my love of St. Augustine were his words, "I believe to better understand". To that can be added that the better we understand the greater our belief. They are special words to me because much effort can be wasted by not believing the written word of God. It is a far better use of our spiritual time to accept and embrace his Word so we can move on to better understanding. In our personal spiritual life the words of St. Augustine not only help us to better understand but to grow our faith.

The final fall of the Western Roman Empire in 476 AD would also influence events within the Church. Although the fall of the Empire was due to a gradual decline in social and economic conditions, invasions by the German clans marked its end. By that time, the Christian religion had become the prominent religion within the region of what had been the Roman Empire. The fall of the Roman Empire also led to greater involvement of the Church in secular governance.

After the fall of the Western Roman Empire, that area would be governed by Germanic rulers. The Eastern Roman Empire would continue under the reign of Constantinople throughout most of the Middle Ages. The Catholic Church as already noted would be influential in the governance of both Empires.

Throughout the Middle Ages, Catholicism was the sole form of Christianity. Since the citizenry of the former Roman Empire had become predominately Catholic, the Church played a significant role in all aspects of society. It would be the builder of parish churches and provide for what education existed. It also played a role in the coronation of rulers during much of that era.

Much could be written about the history of the Church during the Middle Ages, but this book is intended to focus on how people could grow their faith during difficult times. As regards to that capability, life for Christians was much different during the Middle Ages than in the early days of the Church. Wholesale persecutions of Christians had been eliminated and Christians were free to worship and grow their faith as they wished. That was true of what was the "Holy Roman Empire" but not universally true.

One of the most influential Popes of all times, Pope Gregory the Great, sat in the chair of St. Peter from 590 AD to 604 AD. Although a powerful Pope he remained a humble Pope and preferred to be called the "Servant of the Servants of God". From feeding the poor to exercising great authority over both Church and secular government, he deserved the title of "Great". His influence on the governance of the Church has been continued to the present time. Although the structure of "monarchial episcopates" was loosely established early, he strengthened that structure. Archbishops reported to the Pope and Bishops reported to Archbishops. In addition to his many influences within the Church and civil authority he also sent Augustine of Canterbury to convert the Anglo-Saxon people. His influence would be felt by faithful Christians.

Other missionaries in the early Middle Ages would also be influential in spreading the faith. Even as the Middle Ages were beginning, St. Patrick's influence was great in converting the people of present-day Ireland to the Catholic faith. St. Boniface of Germany would do much to spread Christianity to the people of Germany. He was eventually made the Archbishop of Mainz. He was later martyred, an indicator that religious bigotry still existed.

Monks and nuns of the Middle Ages were the workers among the laity. They would establish small parishes in smaller communities and would also be involved in aiding the poor and providing education.

St. Francis of Assisi, who was born in the latter part of the 12th century had a special affinity for helping the poor. He and his followers spent much of their time in that work. St. Francis also had a special love of the Holy Eucharist. His followers still number in the thousands and remain dedicated to aiding the poor.

St. Thomas Aquinas was a renowned philosopher and theologian of the 13th century. His influence remains with the Church and all of us today. He believed that a confluence of faith and reason was necessary for a greater understanding of God.

Some events of Christians during the Middle Ages were not as admirable as the works of the prior two mentioned saints. In 1095, the first Crusade was organized by Pope Urban II. The goal of the Crusade was to drive the Muslims out of Jerusalem and the Holy Land. The last of the Crusades was directed by Emperor Frederick II. The growing strength of Muslim forces won that last battle of the Crusades.

Another questionable goal of those within the Church began in the latter part of the 15th century and would continue for several hundred years. The Spanish Inquisition was begun through the efforts of Queen Isabella I of Castile and Ferdinand II of Aragon. Its purpose was to rid Spain of non-Christians, primarily Jews and Muslims. In the process many non-Christians were tortured or persecuted.

Another Middle Age event that affected Christians in both the Western and Eastern Roman Empire was the Great Schism, which occurred in 1054 AD. It took place under the papacy of Pope Leo IX. The patriarch of Constantinople, Michael Cerularius was not a fan of some of the Western Roman Empire liturgical practices and during his reign he closed a number of Latin churches in Constantinople. That view was further aggravated by Pope Leo's attempt to free southern Italy from the Byzantine Church.

Pope Leo's attempt to free southern Italy had more to do with his desire to claim primacy over all areas of the Church, including Constantinople. The Constantinople patriarch refused that subjugation and that earned him and his party excommunication by Rome. That move was rejected in Constantinople and that led to the Schism, which continues to this day.

As the Middle Ages came to an end, other practices, some corrupt, would lead to the Protestant Reformation. Those practices will be covered in the next chapter along with the reforms which would take place within the Catholic Church.

CHAPTER 3

REFORMATION AND POST-REFORMATION CHURCH

A s we begin this chapter it is good to remember the words of our Lord to St. Peter. *And so I say to you, you are Peter, and upon this rock I will build my church, and the gates of the netherworld shall not prevail against it.* It is good to remember those words because it is the institution that shall not be subjected to failure from the evils of the netherworld. Sadly, those words do not say that human beings within that church shall not be involved in hurting the church. That applies to both the hierarchy and laity.

At the close of the Middle Ages (circa 1500 AD) the church did suffer from many practices that were harmful to the church and needed reform. The papacy had lost prestige. Clergy often were not respected because of their lack of addressing the needs of the people, especially the poor. The Church also was involved with greedy practices, including the selling of tickets for indulgences, whereby those who had the financial resources could "buy" their way into Heaven while the poor could not. All too often religious positions were sold to those who could afford to pay for them. That often led to having priests who were poorly schooled in the beliefs of the Church and led to muddled messages to the laity.

In the year 1515 AD the Pope started a new campaign of selling indulgences to raise money for the modernization of St. Peter's Basilica. This campaign led to the protests of Martin Luther. His major protest concerned the for-sale indulgences because they did not reflect the teaching of our Lord and what had to be done to gain Heaven. Some of his other objections properly protested other abuses of the clergy. My personal view of Luther is that his initial protests were to a large degree legitimate. But as time went on, he became embroiled in disputes, which could better have been voiced privately. On the other side of the coin the Church probably acted too hastily in excommunicating Luther.

Regardless of one's spiritual viewpoints relating to Luther's protests, it was he who initiated the Protestant Reformation, which fairly quickly led to several Protestant religions. It also led to a Reformation of the Catholic Church, which was sorely needed at the time. Many of the reform measures were undertaken at the Council of Trent, which was held during the years of 1545 through 1563 AD. In that period of time 25 sessions were held.

One of the functions of the Council of Trent was to refute some of the Protestant assertions. Most of the other reforms were reassertions and clarifications of prior doctrinal decisions. A major step was the initiation of the Tridentine Mass in Latin which would remain in place for the following 400 years. Other important accomplishments stemming from the Council included the first Catechism of the Catholic Church which was issued in 1566. It would be the first time that all Catholic beliefs would be published in a single document. Subsequently, revisions were also made to the Breviary and Missal. From a personal perspective the affirmation of the transubstantiation of Bread and Wine into the Body and Blood of our Lord was very important, because it is foundational to the Catholic faith.

The Council did not stop the migration of many Catholics to the Protestant religions. There were lost opportunities to negotiate with the Protestant reformers who attended some of the sessions. There was probably too much time spent on points of disagreements instead of agreements. There may also have been too little time spent on matters important to the laity. There is no doubt that the Council of Trent would set the tone for Catholic society in Europe for hundreds of years. After the Council of Trent, the involvement of the Catholic hierarchy in governmental and political affairs would gradually diminish.

Another development of the 16th century was the founding of the Jesuit Order by St. Ignatius Loyola and companions in the year 1534. They would be instrumental in bringing higher education to many of the faithful for many years.

All too often, the hierarchy of the Church have involved themselves in matters of science when the expertise in those matters is lacking. One of those situations occurred to Galileo Galilei, because of his correct view that the earth was in orbit around the sun. For his views, he was subjected to house arrest. Those in the Church better serve the faithful when they confine themselves to matters of faith and morals.

In the Post Reformation era, Christianity and Catholicism would migrate via missionaries to the Americas, Australia, Philippines, and other areas of the world. The apparition of our Lady of Guadalupe would be cause for growing faith and venerating our Blessed Mother, in Mexico and many other parts of the world.

Apparitions by our Blessed Mother would also take place in Lourdes, France - Fatima, Portugal -Knock, Ireland, and other places in the world. To this day millions of Catholics travel to those sites. Thanks to those apparitions in the Post-Reformation era, veneration of our Blessed Mother and faith in our Lord, have increased.

More than 300 years after the Council of Trent ended, Pope Pius IX would open the 1st Vatican Council. The Council was convened over concerns of contemporary ideas associated with the rise of nationalism, liberalism, and materialism. Some of these concerns remain with us in our modern-day societies.

Although such contemporary ideas were the reason for convening the Council, its most significant conclusion related to the declaration of Papal infallibility on matters relating to faith and morals. This is important to the faithful since such dogmas become matters which faithful Catholics must believe.

Several years before the First Vatican Council convened, Pope Pius IX had declared the doctrine of Immaculate Conception for our Blessed Mother. This special Feast Day is celebrated around the world by Catholics. It adds to the veneration of her among faithful Catholics.

The Second Vatican Council would be convened by Pope John XXIII on October 11, 1962. He stated that it was called in "obedience to the Holy Spirit". Following the death of Pope John XXIII, his successor, Pope Paul VI, reconvened the Council which continued until Dec. 8, 1965.

To the faithful the most obvious change was in the Mass. It would begin to be said in the vernacular language instead of Latin, and revisions were made to the Eucharistic prayers. The altars in many Churches were changed so the priest would be facing the people during the Mass. The laity also became participants of the Mass in the form of Lectors and Eucharistic ministers. Some modernization was also done to the liturgical music and artwork. Some of these changes caused some degree of divisiveness but are generally well accepted at this time. The use of the Tridentine Latin Mass was not banned and is still in use to a small degree.

What the Council of Trent and 1st Vatican Council were not able to accomplish in regard to greater dialogue with other religions and a greater ecumenical spirit was accomplished to a greater degree at Vatican II. Pope Paul VI underscored the universal call to greater holiness by stating it was "the most characteristic and ultimate purpose of the teachings of the Council".

Although it has not always received the publicity as other changes made at the Council, the important document Lumen Gentium reaffirmed the importance of the Holy Eucharist to Mass and to our Christian Catholic life. It stated, "The Eucharistic Sacrifice is the source and summit of the Christian life". In this writer's opinion that reaffirmation is too frequently overlooked in the teaching of the Catholic faith at this time.

Something the two Vatican Councils did not do was to closely examine the governance of the Church. Dioceses of the Church retain the official designation of Monarchical Episcopates. It is the belief of this writer that the "Monarchical" aspect deserves review. The current governance is at odds with the principal of "Subsidiarity" which the Church suggests for societal governments. It also does not portray a "humble" governance structure.

This Post-Reformation Church chapter would not be complete without reference to the Baltimore Catechism and the extremely important role the women of religious orders played and continue to play in the teaching of the Catholic faith.

As early as 1829, at the First Provincial Council of Baltimore, the Bishops stated their desire that a Catechism be prepared based on an earlier Catechism (Small Catechism) prepared by Cardinal Bellarmine. It was not until 1885 that the Baltimore Catechism would be published. It would eventually be broken down into several editions. Baltimore Catechism 1 was intended for teaching lower elementary grades while # 2 was used for upper grades. The Baltimore Catechism was an instrumental teaching tool for Catholic students until the late 1960s. It influenced the lives of many Catholic faithful. It did an excellent job of teaching the Catholic faith.

After Vatican II and with the decline of usage in the Baltimore Catechism there was a void left in the teaching of the Catholic faith. It was not until 1992 that the Catechism of the Catholic Church was published. While a compendium has been prepared for adults, there has been no compendium or compendia published for children. That absence of teaching from a standard text has led to a smorgasbord of teaching the Catholic faith. The lack of teaching the Catholic faith to our youth in a standard systematic method is a void which still needs to be filled.

The Baltimore Catechism was not the only useful vehicle employed for teaching the faith. For many years, the Catholic faith was taught to elementary and high school students by very good and holy women in religious orders. Their contribution to growing faith for millions of Catholic youth cannot be overstated.

In many ways they were the shepherds to the lambs. I have often (only partially in jest) said that women make better shepherds than men because they instinctively care for lambs, whereas men focus on the methodology of shepherding.

Polls over recent years indicate that a large majority of young Catholics who are baptized stop practicing their Catholic faith after reaching the age of 21. Polls also indicate that a large majority of Catholics do not believe in the Real Presence of the Holy Eucharist.

It is my belief that the lack of a Catechism for youth together with the lack of nuns to teach the faith have much to do with the polls just noted. Our reasoning is flawed if we expect our younger generations to believe that which has not been taught. This lack of teaching the faith will be covered at greater length in a subsequent chapter.

CHAPTER 4

THE SANCTITY OF LIFE ISSUE

Shortly after my retirement in 1998, it was my desire to devote some of my retirement life to social justice causes. After looking at various issues, I concluded that the devaluation of the sanctity of life ranked at the top of immoral social issues. My decision was influenced by our Country's Declaration of Independence which lists life as the first of the inalienable rights bestowed on us by our God.

I also believed it was a grave spiritual sin because our Lord is not only the Creator of human life, but He also endows every human being with an immortal soul at conception. It was also my view that too little was being done within our Church to promote a greater respect for human life and especially the human soul.

Despite those very basic moral reasons, our country sanctioned human murder with the Roe versus Wade Supreme Court decision in 1973. With that legalization of abortions, we have permitted the deaths of more than 60 million pre-born infants since the Roe versus

Wade decision. That is a national moral tragedy. And yet, despite this moral depravity, polls have indicated that 50 percent and at times more concur with the decision to legalize abortions. Sadly, a large percentage of Catholics also concur.

Abortions, together with the legalization of assisted suicide, are examples of how easily people can fall prey to diabolical intrusions. When a society places its secular values above the values given us by God, that society faces spiritual troubles. In accepting the immoral practice of devaluing human life, our culture ignores that God is the Creator of all things and most certainly human life, including the human soul, which he creates at conception.

Not many acts of human beings against love of neighbor rise to the level of immorality than does the murder of another human being. There is no doubt that abortions and euthanasia are violations of the fifth commandment, despite being sanctioned by our government.

It has been a long-held belief of mine that a major void within our Church and within pro-life groups has been the lack of any emphasis on the importance of the human soul. It is the very special creation of our Lord and abortion deprives that human being the struggles of life which determine its place in eternity. How our Lord deals with that aborted pre-born infant's soul is a mystery to us on earth.

One of the sad fallouts of abortions and euthanasia is that those practices are too often justified or ignored by people who claim to be faithful. Such justifications are, in fact perversions of faith, because they ignore the existence of our Lord's fifth commandment.

On the other hand, there are many wonderful people involved with organizations, which advocate strongly for the sanctity of life. As noted earlier, it would help enhance their position if they advocated more for the importance of the human soul.

In regard to how we deal with the diabolical acts of abortion and euthanasia there is a choice to be made. We can succumb to the diabolical influence within society and try to convince ourselves that if government and a large part of society condone abortions and euthanasia, it must be okay morally. We can also choose to be our Lord's helping hand on earth and proclaim the diabolical evils of abortions and euthanasia.

There are many ways in which we can aid in proclaiming the sanctity of life. As with all things we can pray that others will understand that all lives, born and unborn, are sacred creations of God.

In addition to prayer, there are numerous other ways we can proclaim the sanctity of life. We can and should be willing to tell others that life is a sacred gift of God.

There are also many organizations whom we can support both vocally and financially. The National Right to Life organization has been in existence even before the Roe vs. Wade decision legalized abortions. Priests for Life, under the direction of Father Frank Pavone are also strong advocates of the sanctity of life. A more recently established organization, Students for Life, have been doing excellent work on college campuses.

As people of faith, we have an obligation to proclaim the Word of God. If we wish to grow our faith during the diabolical intrusion of sanctioned abortions, we can do so by being advocates of the sanctity of life. In doing that we are embracing the fifth commandment. When we demonstrate the love of his commandments, we demonstrate a love of our God. It is not always easy to take positions against acts, which are diabolical, and that many embrace, but it is important to do so if we wish to grow in faith.

CHAPTER 5

LACK OF TEACHING THE CATHOLIC FAITH

A t this time in the history of the Catholic Church, it is sad to witness the lack of participation in the Catholic faith especially among our younger generations.

Many reasons have been advanced, which try to explain that lack of participation. Much blame has been pointed toward the clerical sexual abuse scandals. While that may be one of the reasons, it is my personal view that the lack of teaching the Catholic faith is a far more significant reason. I believe that, because one's own personal faith is not and should not be dependent significantly on the faith of others, including the clergy. Of greater significance to my own personal faith and the faith of others is what has been taught about our faith and what we continue to better understand about our faith.

Following Vatican II, two events occurred which I believe have led to a lack of understanding about our Catholic faith.

For many years, the Baltimore Catechism was the major vehicle for teaching our Catholic faith. At the end of the 1960s, that Catechism, for reasons I do not understand, discontinued to hold its position as the primary vehicle for teaching. Sadly, as noted earlier, there has been no Catechism since that time that has been published or endorsed by the US Conference of Catholic Bishops (USCCB) for teaching our youth.

A second factor that began occurring at about the same time, which also has been noted earlier, was the reduction in the number of women entering religious life. It was the good Catholic nuns who had been in the forefront of teaching the Catholic faith to our elementary and high school students.

My reason for believing that the above two factors have much to do with the lack of participation in our Catholic faith has much to do with the belief advanced by St. Paul. Although I am condensing and paraphrasing his words, he told us we cannot expect people to believe that which they have not been taught. Without a prepared or endorsed Catechism by our Bishops and without the nuns who taught us so well, it has proven to be difficult to have a systematic approach to properly teach the Catholic faith.

It may take some effort to have a systematic approach to teaching the Catholic faith, but it is not impossible, and it needs to be done.

For many recent years, the Bishops of our country have simply ignored the need for teaching our Catholic faith in a systematic manner. If by no one else, this writer has brought it to their attention many times, but again for reasons I do not understand they simply ignore that the problem exists. A systematic system is a very basic need to teach our Catholic faith. Diabolical? Probably.

The resolution to the problem may take some effort but the resolution by the Bishops requires only two fairly simple steps:

1. Either prepare a new compendium of the Catechism of the Catholic Church for our youth or endorse one that already exists. The YOUCAT or the new St. Joseph edition of the Baltimore Catechism are both good examples of what could be endorsed.
2. After Step 1 is done, instruct all Parish pastors that the prepared or endorsed Catechisms are the ones that are to be used for teaching the Catholic faith.

The USCCB as well as individual Bishops have had many issues to deal with over recent years, especially the clerical sexual abuse issue. They are also dealing with the issue of the declining number of priests. It is understandable that the lack of teaching the Catholic faith may not be at the top of Bishops' priorities, but in my view it should be. They are the shepherds who succeeded the Good Shepherd and it is their job to feed the lambs. Is it another diabolical intrusion? Maybe.

A greater focus on teaching the Catholic faith merits attention for several other reasons. An increase in faith among the Catholic laity may aid in a greater number of vocations to the priesthood and to religious life.

Another reason to improve the teaching of our Catholic faith relates to the declining number of Catholics who believe in the Real Presence of the Holy Eucharist. The lack of teaching the Catholic faith extends to all the Sacraments and most especially to the Holy Eucharist.

The Holy Eucharist is the centerpiece of the Mass and that in turn makes it the foundation of our Catholic religion. The lack of belief in the Real Presence makes it more difficult to convince our younger generations to practice their faith.

For many years, it has been a project of mine to persuade the Bishops of this country to prepare a compendium or compendia of the Catechism of the Catholic Church for our youth and possibly other groups within the Church. Another option is to endorse the use of Catechisms which already exist, such as the two previously noted in this chapter.

A part of that project was a letter sent to all Diocesan Bishops in this country. Some responded favorably, but as yet the USCCB has not seen the need to either prepare a compendium or endorse specific existing Catechisms. Several responded that YOUCAT can fill the need but until recently an edition for younger elementary grades has not been available.

It remains my strong belief that participation in our Catholic faith could be increased by improved teaching of our faith.

Because of my lack of success in convincing the USCCB and Diocesan Bishops, several years ago I began a mini-ministry of my own to do what I could do to spread the truths of some of the most basic beliefs of our Catholic religion. That ministry includes donating some of my previous books to Catholic book and gift stores around the country. The largest number of books donated were "The Miracle of the Eucharist" and "Toward a Holier Catholic Church". Several others were also included.

In visiting those stores, I soon discovered that a large majority of their owners or managers shared the view that teaching of the Catholic faith needs to be improved.

After reviewing several Catechisms, I believe the new St. Joseph edition of the Baltimore Catechism is a good second choice for teaching our Catholic faith. I also believe YOUCAT is another good choice. My first choice remains an USCCB compendium of our Catechism of the Catholic Church.

It is gratifying to observe that the above referenced new St. Joseph edition of the Baltimore Catechism has become a very popular choice by many Catholics for teaching their youth.

The title of this book addresses the importance of maintaining our faith through diabolical times. Whatever the reason, we know that fewer Catholics are practicing their faith. It has been my belief and it remains my belief that we must do a better job of teaching our Catholic faith.

More than ten years ago, I received a letter from the USCCB expressing their view that adequate teaching materials existed for teaching the faith. That may have been true and may still be true but if such materials are not used, their value does not exist. In any event, after receiving that letter, I dropped the subject for several years.

However, after observing the continuing diminishment in the practice of faith, I decided to become more active in promoting the need for improved catechesis. Hereafter, as long as I believe we have a need to improve the teaching of our Catholic faith, I will continue my mini-ministry project.

CHAPTER 6

CLERICAL SEXUAL ABUSES

For more than the past 25 years, the scandals of clerical sexual abuses have been an ongoing reminder that all human beings are sinners. Despite the damage done to the Church and to themselves, such sinful offenses by members of the clergy should not be used as an excuse to diminish the practice of our own faith. It should also be remembered that a great majority of Bishops and priests are good and holy people.

Even though clerical sexual abuses should not diminish our faith in God, those sins may well be a factor in diminishing participation in the Catholic religion. In saying that I am making a distinction between faith and religion. Inasmuch as faith is a very personal relationship between our soul and God, the sins of others should not be an excuse for diminishing that relationship. On the other hand, the sexual sins of Bishops and priests can be a negative factor in the participation in the practice of Catholic religion. To the extent that happens, those sinful practices are diabolical because the lack of participation in one's religion can hamper an increase in one's faith.

The participation in one's religion and other religious liturgical services are useful in the increase in one's faith. That is particularly true of participation in the Holy Eucharist which links us to the divinity of our Lord.

The message of this book is to stress the importance of maintaining or increasing our faith during diabolical times. The news of clerical sexual abuses should never be used as an excuse for diminishing our faith. It is God, who is the centerpiece of our faith.

Our spiritual faith should be a faith that is strong enough to always understand that we live on earth in order to prepare ourselves for an eternity with our God. That purpose of life should not be diminished by the evils that surround us, including clerical sexual abuses. We can look to the lives of those who were martyred for their faith to reinforce our own faith during diabolical times.

Even though it is my view that clerical sexual abuse should not be an excuse to diminish our faith or participation in our faith, it is nevertheless a scandal. As noted before, those scandals probably have had some impact on the diminished number of people who participate in their faith. That in turn diminishes opportunities to increase people's faith.

Other spiritual harms can also be attributed to clerical sexual abuse cases. They are a very bad example to young men and women, who may be considering a vocation to the priesthood or religious life. In a nation that sorely needs more priests and religious it is harmful.

Another spiritual harm caused by the clerical sexual abuse scandal was the damage it did to our good and holy Bishops and priests. They have, no doubt, been unjustly tarnished by the acts of a small minority of those who strayed from the priestly vow to chastity.

It has also made a target of some good and holy clergy who have had allegations made against them which may not be warranted. The Church has been forced to deny the service of some good priests because of allegations.

I do believe, as Bishop Barron put it, that the clerical sexual abuse scandal is diabolical. In recent years, the Church has been subjected to diabolical intrusions. The lack of participation in the Catholic faith and the lack of belief in the Real Presence of the Holy Eucharist have been attributed by many to the clerical sexual abuses. As already stated, I do not believe that for faithful Catholics, those situations should be laid solely at the foot of clerical sexual abuse. My reasons for that have already been covered in this book.

CHAPTER 7

PERPETUAL SINFUL TEMPTATIONS

I n the prior chapters we have tried to demonstrate specific situations which were diabolical and also sinful to human beings or may have led to sins by others. We live in a world where such situations surround us constantly. In order to achieve our goal of living eternally in our Lord's kingdom we need to be aware of and resist all types of temptations.

As noted earlier in this book, the best antidote to temptation is prayer. When we pray, we also are fighting against temptations to sin. The world is filled with evil and has been filled with evil since the first sins in the Garden of Eden.

In the 6th chapter of Matthew, our Lord reminded his followers that focusing on the present time is of importance, and that worrying about yesterday and tomorrow is fruitless. He told us that things of the earth are what pagans seek and that we are better served when we *seek first the kingdom of God and his righteousness, and all these things* (earthly needs) *will be given you besides. Do not worry about tomorrow; tomorrow will take care of itself. Sufficient for a day is its own evil.*

It is not an easy task to perpetually seek the things of God, because we are surrounded by the things of this earth. Our sinful pride is at the root of our sinfulness. When we place our earthly desires above the things of God, we expose our self to things of evil. Yes, sufficient for every day is its own evil.

Except for our Blessed Mother, all human beings have been and are sinners. The lack of humility and kindness stand in the path of the two greatest commandments our Lord gave us. In order to love our Lord with all our heart, soul, mind, and strength, we must be humble. And to love our neighbor as our self we must be kind. Those two perpetual problems may not cause grievous sin, but they cause sin nonetheless.

It is difficult for any human being to go through an entire day totally focused on God, but it takes that total perpetual focus to fully observe his first command. How many of us can honestly say that we can go through an entire day much less an entire lifetime constantly focused on God and the things of God. Even Peter when put to the test failed and the cock did crow. David failed in his lust of Bathsheba. All of us fail. But we must try. The more time we dedicate to God the better we observe that first great commandment. We are told to pray constantly. To pray constantly is to love God constantly. It is a very difficult and never-ending goal.

It is also difficult for humans to go through a day being kind to everyone at all times. But if we are to love our neighbor as our self that too must be a goal. There is nothing wrong with loving our self, but we must love our God more than our self and we are commanded to also love our neighbor as our self.

When we closely examine our conduct at the end of each day, we can better understand our Lord's words that sufficient for each day is its own evil. The underlying reason for humans' lack of humility and kindness, is our original sin of pride. When that pride focuses on our self rather than on God and neighbor, we violate the two great commandments He gave us, and we sin.

Those two great commandments He gave us were the positive way of stating what the Ten Commandments told us not to do. But the Ten Commandments give us the things from which we must refrain in order to be better observers of the two great commandments.

The first of the Ten Commandments provides a good example of things we need to observe to better love our God. When we put other gods ahead of the one, true God we fail. It is not just the molten calf of the Old Testament that represents false gods. It is obsession of putting earthly things above God. That includes an obsession for money, obsessive desires of bigger and better homes and cars, and other earthly things. God must be our focus.

As we gradually grow to accept and practice what the Ten Commandments forbid us to do, we also gradually grow to love those commandments and as we grow to love them, we also grow in love of He who gave us those commandments. In John 14:15 Jesus told us, "If you love me, you will keep my commandments".

I believe an excellent practice for everyone is the evening Examen, which St. Ignatius Loyola gave us. It is good to reflect each evening on how we spent our day and on how we observed or failed to observe the two great commandments.

We have a number of ways we can do that. How well we did relative to each of the Ten Commandments has already been noted. Other tests are available. We can also measure our actions and thoughts against the seven deadly sins of pride, greed, envy, wrath, lust, gluttony and sloth. As already noted, it is pride that leads to all other sins. It was the sin that led Eve to eat of the forbidden fruit.

If we wish to look at the positive side of our personal ledger, we can spend time reflecting on how well we did in observing the Beatitudes which are listed in the first chapter. When we say the Penitential Act at Mass, we ask for forgiveness on the things we "have failed to do".

We are sinners and because we are sinners, we need God's never-ending forgiveness and mercy. He has already earned our salvation by his death on the cross, but the way we live our life is the key to how we will spend our eternal life.

Yes, the sins of pride and kindness and others noted in this chapter are sins humans have committed since the beginning of time and will continue to commit.

But our Lord gave us some goals to try to achieve. We will never be perfect observers of his two great commandments, but we have the perpetual goal to keep trying.

CHAPTER 8

LEGALIZING HUMAN LIFE DEVALUATION

I n an earlier chapter of this book we addressed the sanctity of life issue from the standpoint of shortcomings within our Church and pro-life organizations. In this chapter we will address the same issue from the shortcomings within our country.

This country was founded on the belief that the first inalienable right granted by God to human beings was life. That belief was the basis of many state laws, which outlawed abortions, for most of the first 200 years of this nation. When the inalienable right to life is set aside, our country slides down the slippery slope of immorality. It does not matter what reasons are presented to justify the legalization of killing a human being, because none can replace the fact that the beginning and end of human life is a matter of God's domain.

In the 1973 decision of Roe versus Wade the Supreme Court ignored the inalienable right of life, when it decided that a Texas law outlawing abortion was not constitutional, and in so doing, legalized abortions. No prior or subsequent Supreme Court decision has ever been worse. It simply sanctioned murder. It permitted one human being to terminate the life of another human being and used the right to privacy as an excuse to justify their decision.

Justice Byron White, who was a member of the Supreme Court at the time Roe versus Wade was decided, dissented in the case. In his dissent he stated the following: *With all due respect, I dissent. I find nothing in the language or history of the Constitution to support the Court's judgment. The Court simply fashions and announces a new constitutional right for pregnant mothers and, with scarcely any reason or authority for its action, invests that right with sufficient substance to override most existing state statutes … As an exercise of raw judicial power the Court perhaps has authority to do what it does today, but in my view, its judgment is an improvident and extravagant exercise of the power of judicial review that the Constitution extends to this Court.*

Many years ago, in my first book, "Redefining Morality – A Threat to our Country" I noted that it was my view that Justice White did not go far enough. I do not believe that the Supreme Court has the authority to find or announce a "new constitutional right" for anyone. That role belongs to Congress and the American people. And, it certainly did not have the moral right to decide that it had the power to overturn the Fifth Commandment our God gave to Moses – "Thou shalt not kill". As a result of the Supreme Court decision, our country has legally permitted tens of millions of unborn infants to be killed. It is a moral travesty that has devalued the sanctity of human life.

As I am writing this chapter, our country is in the midst of a pandemic referred to as coronavirus. Many thousands of people will suffer death as a result of the virus during this calendar year. There is no doubt that it is a tragedy. It is also a tragedy that a recent source estimated that 42 million abortions were performed worldwide in 2019. It will be left to our Lord to judge which is the greater moral tragedy.

Earlier I noted the danger of going down a slippery slope once "sanctioned murder" is permitted. In recent years, several states have authorized euthanasia and have called such sanctioned, murderous acts, actions respecting the dignity of life. When violating our Lord's Fifth Commandment and then classifying it as respecting the dignity of life, we insult our Creator.

When the government sanctions immoral practices it leads its citizens to accept such sanctioning as being an acceptable moral practice. When such secular reasoning replaces the moral laws our Lord gave us, we trespass against his commandments.

When a society subordinates the laws of God to the laws of humans, that society begins decaying from within. One need only study the decline of the Roman Empire to verify such decay. In our country today far too many practices are being accepted which depart from the Word of God.

But such flaws in a society do not stop good people from maintaining and growing their faith. Following the Roe versus Wade decision, groups began forming which would become referred to as "pro-life" organizations. We noted several of those organizations in Chapter 4.

It is my view, history will not be kind to this period of sanctioned murders that take place in this nation and other nations which permit the killing of preborn infants. While I applaud the aforementioned organizations whose purpose is to protect all human life from conception to natural death, I do not extend that applause to other institutions of this country who should also be at the forefront of decrying this affront to the inalienable God given right to life.

The devaluation of life via abortions and euthanasia together with a society that accepts those immoral behaviors says something about that society. One thing it certainly says, as noted earlier, is that the wishes of God have been overlooked. In such a society other immoral actions become more commonplace. In this country, there has been a serious breakdown of the family and more and more children are without two parents. Drugs become more widespread. Immoral language becomes more commonplace. Hatred and divisiveness begin replacing love of God and neighbor. Secular laws become more important than the laws of God.

A society that ignores God and his commandments is indeed a society that is in trouble.

CHAPTER 9

BIGOTRY, HATRED AND DIVISIVENESS

Throughout the history of mankind, scientific advances have been made steadily, which reveal more and more of God's creation. When scientists credit God with all creation they perform a good service for their own and future generations. Unfortunately, that is not always the case. Too many in their scientific achievements, do not credit their discoveries to the magnificence of our Creator. It is a lack of humility that leads humans to think their scientific discoveries are a credit to the work of humans instead of the work of God.

Human intelligence is a good thing if it is accompanied by the understanding that such intelligence is also attributable to our Creator. Such understanding comes from spiritual wisdom, which is an attribute of the immortal soul. Unfortunately, we are all sinners and throughout the course of human history, the sins of pride have manifested themselves in many ways and humans thereby demonstrate their reliance on human intelligence instead of spiritual wisdom.

Bigotry throughout human history is one of the flaws of human thought when spiritual wisdom is ignored. Loving our neighbor as our self is the second of the greatest commandments Jesus gave us. After loving Him no commandment is greater than love of neighbor. During his time on earth our Lord asked that we love our neighbor as He loved us. We always fall short of that goal.

Bigotry is not an area in which humans have made great achievements as has been done in the scientific area. The Old and New Testaments are filled with examples when humans have loved themselves far more than their neighbors. But in this section of our book we are looking at shortcomings in our nation.

Bigotry has always been a problem in this country just as it has always been since the creation of flawed human beings. I do not know if we can say it has been particularly worse in any period of our nation than it is today.

There is no question that the early settlers of this nation, did not always treat Native Americans as they treated one another. There is also no question that slaves of African descent were treated inhumanely. But we can also find incredibly good people in those who founded our nation. Those early settlers and founders of this nation were guilty of treating Native American and African Americans with less respect than they treated themselves. But those same founders were also the ones who in the Declaration of Independence recognized the inalienable rights of life, liberty and the pursuit of happiness endowed on humans by their Creator.

Are we less bigoted as a nation today? We have certainly corrected some wrongs in recognizing the human rights of Native American, African American. immigrants from some other countries as well as women. On the flip side, other forms of bigotry have come into being. Name calling together with finger-pointing is now being used regularly to denigrate other people and other groups of people. "Racists", "Misogynists", are among the many terms now being used in a bigoted fashion to belittle others. Those using such terms are themselves the ones who promote bigotry. They do not portray a love of neighbor.

Bigotry of different cultures and different nationalities has not disappeared from this earth. It is the arrogance of anyone or any group to assume they are superior to any other person or group. Our Lord warned us not to judge others. That is also something that is in his Domain. Our job is to love one another.

In recent years, our nation has been plagued by signs of greater hatred and divisiveness. That is especially true in the political arena and in our news media. Too often in those areas, peaceful and harmonious disagreements are a thing of the past. It is my strong belief that such hatred and divisiveness occurs, when the love of God and neighbor are subordinated to greed, power and arrogance. When love of God and neighbor are removed, sinful pride manifests itself in sinful ways.

In my younger years, it was hard to detect the political leanings of news anchors. During their working lives I was not aware of the political party affiliations of Howard Smith, Walter Cronkite, Chet Huntley or David Brinkley during their working lives. They were the news anchors of ABC, CBS and NBC, the major TV networks of that time. It was only after they retired that I learned of their political leanings.

During that period of time one could depend on getting objective news, without the political views of those outstanding anchors. That was also truer of the newspapers at that time. Today, the political views have become more dominant than the facts, regarding the news. It is sad and also reflected in the poor ratings of the media. Why they find a benefit in skewing the news to their political views is hard to understand. In skewing the news they harm their ratings, which one would think a wise person would want to improve. But in this period of time, objectivity and wisdom are lacking in too much of the news media. A country is harmed when citizens cannot rely on the objectivity of the news media. Eventually, as has happened, people no longer trust the news media. Their low standings in polls testify to that.

But as within many difficult situations there are some in news media who rise above the general indictment of the media. Blanket indictments are rarely true.

This book is about people growing faith. Does that relate to news? In my view the answer is yes. Why? Because good news reporters understand that truthfulness and objectivity are what God expects of humans. When news reporting is truthful and objective, the trust of people in the news increases.

Another area of our country that suffers from hatred and divisiveness is the political area. Politics has always been and probably will always be an area of some acrimony. However, in recent years such acrimony is becoming far more divisive. The greed associated with maintaining power has too frequently become more important than taking care of the people they should be serving.

Politicians, who hold elective national offices, now spend more time raising money for their political races than they do in representing their constituents. That alone is an indictment of the political situation today. In addition to that, members of the Senate and House of Representatives spend a great deal of time in recess. The time spent on raising money and in recess does not allow much time for legislative matters. And much of the time spent on legislative matters in the current era is spent on denigrating the ideas of the opposition party. Why? The lust for power together with the absence of faith in God and neighbor are not a winning combination for representing their constituents.

As is true with the news media, it would be wrong to paint all in Congress with being more concerned with their own power than taking care of the welfare of the

American people. Unfortunately, such good people no longer seem to be a majority in our nation's capital.

Bigotry, hatred and divisiveness are not good indicators of a healthy society. Love of God, love of neighbor and a selfless interest in both are good indicators of a healthy society.

CHAPTER 10

RESTRICTING FREEDOM OF RELIGION

O ur founding fathers were an exceptional group of people when it came to understanding the importance of freedom to individuals and the role God plays in extending that freedom to human beings. The Declaration of independence captured that understanding in its opening words:

When in the course of human Events, it becomes necessary for one People to dissolve the Political Bands which have connected them with another, and to assume among the Powers of the Earth, the separate and equal Station to which the Laws of Nature and of Nature's God entitle them, a decent Respect to the Opinions of Mankind requires that they should declare the causes which impel them to the Separation.

We hold these Truths to be self-evident that all Men are created equal, that they are endowed by their Creator with certain unalienable Rights, that among these are Life, Liberty, and the Pursuit of Happiness...

The words following the above opening of the Declaration go on to say that if such rights are abused by government, the people have the right to alter or abolish it and to form a new government.

In the 245 years since the Declaration was written, governments at both the federal and state levels have grown tremendously and as Thomas Jefferson warned; as government grows, liberty yields. Liberty has indeed yielded in this country through the imposition of a preponderance of laws and regulations, that rarely get terminated. Several years ago I published a book "The Transformation of America – As Government Grows, Liberty Yields", in which I detail many of the dangers to this country as government has grown and become more intrusive in the lives of its citizens.

Over the past 245 years, that growth in government has not only been intrusive into the lives of citizens but has begun becoming intrusive in religions. Before examining some of such intrusiveness, let us take a look at what the Constitution says in the First Amendment:

Congress shall make no law respecting an establishment of religion, or prohibiting the free exercise thereof; or abridging the freedom of speech, or of the press, or the right of the people peaceably to assemble, and to petition the Government for a redress of grievances.

The words so frequently used to describe the First Amendment as regards religion are "separation of Church and State". Those words were first used by Thomas Jefferson in 1802 and were part of a private letter he had written. There is a small but significant difference between the words of the First Amendment and the words used by Jefferson. The First Amendment very specifically states that there shall be "no law respecting an establishment of religion or prohibiting the free exercise thereof". For most of the first 175 years of this country the relationship between government and religions was very harmonious. But in the middle of the 20th century things began changing.

Until the middle of the 20th century, prayer in public schools was widely accepted and practiced. Since that time, prayer in public schools has become banned based on the First Amendment. That makes no common or legal sense. First of all prayer is not specifically only a religious exercise. Prayer is a practice of people conversing with their Creator. Prayer is not specific to any religion, nor is prayer related to only those belonging to religions. If a law did exist which prohibits prayer because it could be viewed as a religion (which it is not) it would be unconstitutional because, "no law is permitted which prohibits the free exercise" of religion. To deny prayer anywhere including schools, is simply the usurpation of the First Amendment.

The denial of prayer began a series of Supreme Court decisions that had far more to do with a majority of the Court's members indicating their secular desire to diminish the practice of faith by good people than it did with upholding the First Amendment of the Constitution.

In 1980 the Supreme Court indicated their willingness to establish an unconstitutional anti-faith bias, when they disallowed a Kentucky law that required the display of the Ten Commandments. While the Kentucky law may have been excessively aggressive in its demands, it did nothing wrong, because their law did not relate to any specific religion. The Ten Commandments are not the commands of any specific religion. The Supreme Court had no more of a need to strike down the law than it does to strike down the words in the Declaration of Independence which speak to "the Laws of Nature and of Nature's God" and again when it notes the rights of citizens, "that they are endowed by their Creator with certain unalienable rights, that among these are Life, Liberty, and the Pursuit of Happiness". Rather than a decision upholding the First Amendment, the Court again was attempting to diminish the symbols that are important to people of faith.

The decisions the Supreme Court made regarding prayer and the Ten Commandments should never have been heard by the Court. It was a very long stretch to rule that prayer and the Ten Commandments were somehow tied to the First Amendment. It would be more accurate to say that those decisions were diabolically inspired.

But the highest court in the land continued to hear cases and make decisions that would further discourage the display of faith by God-fearing and God-loving people, including people of faith who were not necessarily associated with any specific religion. It is difficult to find any rationale for them that is not diabolical.

In 1989, the Court made another decision that was related to Christian religions in general but again not related to any specific Christian religious denomination. In this case the Court decided that the display of the Christmas creche on the grounds of a county courthouse was not permissible under the establishment clause of the First Amendment. There was no law that had been established in the case (Allegheny County vs. ACLU). The Supreme Court had no right and certainly no need to hear the case because there was no law that was violated.

The highest court in this land, through a lack of interpreting the proper meaning of the word religion, has used the Constitution against people of faith beyond that intended by the founding fathers. It has been most unfortunate that good constitutionalists were not in numbers on the Court to negate those judges who in effect were using the Constitution to discriminate against people of faith, which was exactly what the First Amendment intended to protect.

But faith in God is a powerful influence on human beings. Under Communist rule in the former Soviet Union, efforts were made to stifle religion and religious practices. But today after many decades of Communist rule, Eastern European countries are now among the most faithful in all of Europe. When governments attempt to oppress religion, many faithful grow in faith. It is possible for governments to make attempts to dissuade people from practicing their religion, but governments cannot eliminate the growth of faith in the human soul. Governments would be well-served to accept the views of faith held by the founding fathers of this country and set forth in the Declaration of Independence. The God-given right to the "pursuit of happiness" is a right that extends to the practice of religion and that pursuit should never be stifled by governments.

CHAPTER 11

LIVING THROUGH THE CORONAVIRUS PANDEMIC OF 2020

This chapter of the book was not included in my original outline, which I began in the fall of 2019. At that time, the coronavirus outbreak had not spread to this country. But as this chapter is being written (early part of 2020), it has become a deadly virus around the world. It has not only caused death, but it has caused many to lose their jobs and most of the people in this country and the rest of the world to lead a different and sheltered lifestyle.

But it has also been a time of reflection for many and a time to assess their faith in God. A recent poll indicated that many have indeed acknowledged that their faith in God has grown during the pandemic.

Faith is a gift from God and is our human response to God. God has revealed himself through his Creation, and most especially through his Son, Jesus Christ.

The words from the beginning of the Catechism of the Catholic Church are worth remembering during times such as this pandemic:

The desire for God is written in the human heart, because man is created by God and for God; and God never ceases to draw man to himself. Only in God will he find the truth and happiness he never stops searching for: The dignity of man rests above all on the fact that he is called to communion with God. This invitation to converse with God is addressed to man as soon as he comes into being. For if man exists, it is because God has created him through love, and through love continues to hold him in existence...

God's ways are mysterious. He gives humans a free will and lets them choose if and how they wish to seek and converse with Him. The poll noted above is an encouraging sign that in the solitude of our homes, during a pandemic, people can grow their faith.

There are many ways we have in our homes to grow our faith. Jesus himself suggested going to our rooms and praying in silence. In this day of advanced communications we can stream Masses on our computer or watch them on TV. We have an innumerable amount of ways to grow our faith in the solitude of our home.

It is a good time to reflect on the wonders of our Creator and his Creations. Man has never been able to explain adequately the origin of Creation in earthly terms and without recognizing that our Almighty Father created from nothing man will never be able to explain it. We can reflect on the endless expanse of our universe and all that is in it. We can ponder the eternity of time. We can wonder how much our Almighty Father controls the things He created or how much he lets nature run its own course. From where does weather begin and from where do the winds originate and end? There is no end to the amazement and exultation of all his creation. The more we believe in Him as Creator of all, the better we will come to understand.

The solitude of our homes also provides the opportunity to better understand the great love the Son of God, Jesus Christ, has for all humans. He humbled himself to come to earth as a human and to couple his divine nature with his human nature. He led a humble life while on earth and taught people what they need to know to enjoy eternity with Him. He accepted great suffering and death on a cross to redeem the sins of mankind. He rose from the dead on the third day to demonstrate his divinity. He remained on earth another forty days after his Resurrection to continue teaching, and to send forth his Apostles and disciples to proclaim what he had taught. He then sent the Holy Spirit to dwell among us and to show us the right path.

If the pandemic is accepted in a manner that will bring all of us closer to our God, then it may help accomplish that which St. Paul told us. Where evil abounds grace abounds even more.

God gives us all a free will. We can choose to reciprocate his great love for us as best we can. He also permits us to deny his existence and reject his teachings. He permits us to choose our place in eternity.

His ways are indeed mysterious. As noted earlier, we do not know how much or how little he chooses to control his non-human creations. We do not understand why pandemics such as the coronavirus are permitted by God to exist. He may well permit a great deal of his creation to exist in a natural earthly manner. The pandemic may have been a creation by those who have a free will. God does not stop humans from being evil and maybe He also does not stop earthquakes, floods, pandemics and other tragedies to freely happen naturally or by humans.

Sacred Scripture does tell us that God sent the plagues to Egypt during the time of Moses. He sent the deadly serpents to kill many during the Exodus. He also sent the rains that created the great flood, which destroyed the living creatures on the earth during the time of Noah.

We do not know God's ways. Could he have been instrumental in sending the coronavirus pandemic? Yes. Did he? We do not know.

But if we use this time of sheltering-in-place as a time to grow our faith, our spiritual wisdom, and our holiness, then grace will have abounded even more than the evil which brought us earthly human tragedy.

If the coronavirus is a reminder that faith-based morality is the morality that best models our Lord and Savior, then the sacrifices made of living through the pandemic will have been worth it for our society.

CHAPTER 12

ACCEPTANCE OF IMMORAL PRACTICES

When a society turns away from faith in God it also tends to ignore his commands. Secular commands begin replacing God's commands. In such an environment those with the most power, especially those in government, establish the practices of such a society. But it is not only government that participates in establishing the mores of a society. In a democracy, it is the people who also elect those who participate in establishing the beliefs and practices of the society. As more people accept secular commands, culture begins changing as it accepts less of what God wills and more of humanistic secular reasoning.

In the United States, there has been an evolving movement away from the beliefs our founding fathers had for establishing a new nation. We have already recited the words of the Declaration of Independence and that document left little doubt of how a nation needs to rely on the "self-evident" rights given us by God, if it wishes to be a nation that deserves to exist.

The moral standards of this country have not only evolved away from the beliefs of our founding fathers, but they have also evolved away from the moral standards God has provided. When this country was founded the moral standards of God and country were very closely aligned.

Over the many years that I have been writing on spiritual matters, I have broken down moral standards into three categories:

Faith-based morality – The morality provided us by God through Sacred Scriptures

Religion-based morality – The morality specific to individual religions of the world

Secular-based morality -The morality established by the governments and societies of individual countries

It is my view that the perfect observance of faith-based morality would provide us with Heaven on earth. Because this country was founded based in large part on the principles of faith-based morality it was a great country when it most closely observed faith-based morality. But as already pointed out earlier it has always had its faults (slavery, treatment of Native Americans, treatment of women, etc.). Humans are also sinners, so the perfection of faith-based morality is not found on earth.

But the further a society moves away from faith-based morality, the greater the moral problems that exist in that society. Faith-based morality has the Word of God as its solid foundation. Secular-morality on the other hand has no foundation, except the laws of the country which are put in place by those holding power.

The family is the backbone of all good societies. When there is deterioration in the make-up of the family, it is often accompanied by a breakdown in faith-based morality. It is through the family that the morality of God is passed on from generation to generation. For most of this country's history, the definition of family included a mother and a father as heads of the family household. In recent generations that type of family has diminished as a percent of the country's population. More children than ever are being raised in single-parent settings. That breakdown in family harms a country and the morality of a country since it is a deviation from faith-based morality.

The definition of marriage has changed in this country. For centuries it was always assumed that marriage was between a man and woman. That is no longer the case in this country, and marriage is now permitted, based solely on secular morality.

Drugs of all types, especially opioids, are being consumed by far too many individuals in this country and the number of deaths from overdoses of drugs has reached tragic levels. When God is removed from our daily lives we fruitlessly look elsewhere for happiness.

In a country that looks more to secular morality than to faith-based morality, love of God and love of neighbor begin to be replaced by hatred and divisiveness. The pursuit of power, in the absence of understanding that all power is given to us by God, becomes a ruthless obsession. In recent years, the pursuit of power among politicians has become the end game when the welfare of citizens should be the goal. In that pursuit, politicians display the worst of the political system. Bitter partisanship becomes the main subject of government.

When a culture begins down the road of secular morality, the tendency to belittle faith-based morality becomes part of the societal discourse. We have already noted in a prior chapter the many ways that those in powerful positions begin interpreting the First Amendment in ways it was never intended to be used. The justification is the ever-evolving secular moral standards that have no foundation and continue to evolve.

The indicators of secularism can be found in the growing number of people in this country who claim no religious association. It can also be found in less participation in religious denominations by many who do claim religious association.

Those who continue to find faith-based morality as the best of all moral standards will continue to be those who also demonstrate the greatest love of God and neighbor. It is that love and the growth in their faith-based belief that will best prepare them for their home with Him who is love.

CHAPTER 13

IGNORING CHURCH SHORTCOMINGS

People are sinners and not perfect. Institutions, because they are run by sinful humans, also have shortcomings. Over the past thirty years the shortcomings of those within the Catholic Church have frequently made the news and far too many of them deservedly so.

Chapter 6 of this book was devoted to the issue of clerical sexual abuses and there is no need to examine that sadness to our religion any further. Many blame that issue for the lack of participation in Mass attendance and other liturgical services. In my opinion, that is only one of several issues that are the cause of that lack of participation as well as the lack of belief in the Real Presence of the Holy Eucharist. We have covered some of my own beliefs as the reasons for those shortcomings earlier in this book.

None of the shortcomings of the Church provide an excuse for any individual to ignore the Church Christ himself founded. He understood the shortcomings of those who would govern his Church. He reminded St. Peter that our first Pope would deny him three times before the cock crowed. He selected St. Paul to be one of his greatest followers despite Paul's background as a persecutor of early Christians.

If our faith is dependent on the shortcomings of others, then our faith is shallow. It is not our job to judge the actions of others. That is God's job. Our job is to love the Lord our God with all our heart, soul, mind and strength. Judging others also diminishes the love of our neighbor. Focusing on the faults of others, including the hierarchy of the Church, is a detrimental practice, if we wish to increase our faith.

Complaining and focusing on the faults of others is a useless exercise. It accomplishes nothing and it detracts from the time that could otherwise be spent on the positive ways of loving God and neighbor.

Our faith is a mystery. At the beginning of the Catechism of the Catholic Church, faith is defined in the following manner:

Faith is man's response to God, who reveals himself and gives himself to man, at the same time bringing man a superabundant light as he searches for the ultimate meaning of life.

It is in humility that we better understand our divine God. Faith in God is not dependent on the behavior of others. But that faith must first be taught. As noted earlier in this book, we cannot expect people to know what they have not been taught. Once taught, it is every human being's personal responsibility to grow in faith. If we think our faith is dependent only on our personal beliefs rather than on the understanding that we also need the Holy Spirit to direct us we limit our understanding of our Creator. It is through humility, not selfish pride, that we are able to grow in faith.

In the Church of today, we have too frequently overlooked the first step in spreading faith. It is a duty of the Church and of parents to teach that faith to our youth. If the Church expects a greater understanding of the doctrines of the Catholic faith it must improve its teaching of those doctrines.

All of us by our Baptism, are candidates for proclaiming the Word of God. There are reasons that too many do not practice their faith and do not believe in the Real Presence of the Holy Eucharist. If we believe proclaiming the Word of God and the wonderful benefits of participating in our faith can be helped by our words and actions, then we should be proclaiming those spiritual benefits for others to help them grow their faith.

As noted earlier, it is my belief that the Church needs to publish a compendium of the Catechism of the Catholic Church for teaching our youth. If the Bishops Conference does not wish to publish such a compendium it should at least endorse a Catechism such as "The New Saint Joseph Baltimore Catechism" or "YOUCAT". As noted earlier, both are good catechisms for teaching the faith.

Once that teaching is better standardized within the Church, it is the responsibility of parents to ensure their children receive such education. Sacred Scripture along with catechesis are the basic vehicles that all Catholic Christians need to understand their faith and their Church.

Once that basic teaching takes place it is the individual's personal relationship with God that helps him/her grow in faith and better see the "super abundant light as he searches for the ultimate meaning of life". Focusing on the shortcomings of other sinners within the Church does not assist in seeking that light.

There are many ways to help us grow in our faith. For Catholics, attendance at Mass together with reception of the Holy Eucharist, is what our Lord asked that we "Do this in memory of me". The Eucharist is the ultimate way we have while on earth to be in "Holy Communion" with our Divine Savior. We have many other ways to grow our faith. The Adoration of the Blessed Sacrament is a special way to spend time with our Lord. When not in Church, we can pray in many ways. We can pray the Rosary and the Divine Mercy Chaplet. We can pray in many other ways including many intentions and petitions.

We can also pray that our Church will correct the shortcomings noted in this book. We are all sinners and while the "gates of hell shall not prevail" against our Church, we need to pray for our Pope, Bishops, priests, laity and all Christians. It is far better to pray for them than to focus on their shortcomings. All of us have shortcomings. It is far better to be concerned with the "timber" in our own eyes, than the "splinters" in the eyes of others.

CHAPTER 14

IGNORING OUR COUNTRY'S FAULTS

Much has changed in this country since the signing of the Declaration of Independence. Some of the negative aspects of those changes have been covered in prior chapters of this book.

Through most of its history this country has been a proud defender of freedom around the world. Many courageous young men and women gave their lives for that freedom in World War I and II. This country also fought a Civil War that ended slavery.

After life, liberty is the second mentioned right cited in the Declaration of Independence. We attribute those rights to God, who bestows those rights on all human beings. When those freedoms are given the highest priority of government, then government does its job of putting the care and interest of its citizens where it belongs.

In Chapter 9 we discussed the bigotry, hatred and divisiveness that exists in our country today. Sadly, it exists at the highest level of our government. In recent years political partisanship and personal vindictiveness have become commonplace. Some committees of Congress now do little else other than investigate political rivals.

The media, which has also been mentioned earlier, has become part of the advocacy groups of political parties, instead of objective presenters of the news. Objective journalism has become a thing of the past. In the process the news we get is little more than opinions on the views they wish to advance. Unfortunately, such biased views relate primarily to their preference of people in government and with very little if any objectivity.

The all-too absence of faith-based moral standards extends to the judicial system of our government. It is difficult to find anything but secular morality in the case of Dred Scott, which basically categorized slaves of African American descent as "personal property", instead of human beings who deserved freedom. The Roe versus Wade decision noted earlier, cannot find any justification in faith-based morality. We have also already noted the Supreme Court decisions, which restricted faith-based prayers and symbols on the false pretense that they were "religious" symbols.

If there is any advice I would give to those who vote to elect our public officials, it would be to ignore personalities and focus on the public policy being advanced. It is public policy that matters. Elected government officials come and go.

As is true with our religious leaders, we should also not let our political leaders dictate our personal faith if they act against faith-based morality. There are far too many people I know who let their political views sway their faith. That is sad and that is wrong. It should be our faith that helps us decide how to vote for our public officials. It should also be our faith that is maintained and grown despite what government or our culture may prioritize above faith-based morality.

Neither hierarchy of the Church nor government officials have jurisdiction over our thoughts and over our souls. Our purpose in life is to love our God above all else. If we have faith and grow that faith in him, we will understand how we are to live our lives. That is not only this author's view. That is what our Lord told us during his time on earth. In the 14th chapter of the Gospel of John, our Lord gave us the following words:

Amen, amen, I say to you, whoever believes in me will do the works that I do, and will do greater ones than these, because I am going to the Father.

There are no better words that our Lord gave us to believe in Him and to love Him with all our heart, soul, mind and strength. If we do that, we will love our neighbor and do the good works he wishes us to do. The words He gave us are the words that should guide us and are the reasons our faith in Him should grow. Our faith should not be dependent on the secular words and actions of other human beings.

It is not secular-based morality that will lead us to do the works that He did, but rather, faith-based morality. Our Lord did not leave us on our own when he spoke the words noted above. He said these works would be greater because He was going to the Father. When he left us and went to the Father, He also sent us the Holy Spirit to dwell among us. If we believe in Him and follow the guidance of the Holy Spirit, we can indeed do the works He did. This is what He and the Father wish us to do on earth. Those good deeds we can do on earth are spelled out in the Beatitudes He gave us.

If you wish to follow the words that will help us to grow in our faith, read the Sacred Scriptures and use them as your guide to the way you live your life. Pray often and practice your faith. And pray that He will give you the graces and blessings to grow your faith. He is the Way, the Truth and the Life.

ABOUT THE AUTHOR

George E Pfautsch spent most of his working life as a financial executive for a major forest products and paper company. His final years at Potlatch Corporation were spent as the Senior Vice President of Finance and Chief Financial Officer. Following his retirement, he began writing and speaking about the national morality he believes was intended for this nation by the founding fathers of the country.

He is the author of thirteen previous books that deal with the subjects of morality, justice and faith. He is the co-author of a book written by Melitta Strandberg, which is the story of her family's quest for freedom, before, during and after World War II. He is also the co-author of a book written by Leroy New, the "Guitar Wizard" of Branson, Missouri.

He is married to Dodi, his wife of 59 years. They have two children and four grandchildren.

Printed in the United States
by Baker & Taylor Publisher Services